Vampire Bats

Vampire Bats

Patrick Merrick

THE CHILD'S WORLD®, INC.

Library of Congress Cataloging-in-Publication Data
Merrick, Patrick.
Vampire bats / by Patrick Merrick.
p.   cm.
Includes index.
Summary: Describes the physical characteristics,
behavior, habitat, and life cycle of vampire bats.
ISBN 1-56766-636-1 (lib. reinforced : alk. paper)
1. Vampire bats—Juvenile literature.
[1. Vampire bats. 2. Bats.]   I. Title.
QL737.C52M47   1999
599.4—dc21   98-37312
CIP
AC

Photo Credits

ANIMALS ANIMALS © Michael Fogden: 2
© Bill Johnson: 30
© Jim Clare/BBC Natural History Unit: 6, 24
© Kenneth W. Fink/Bruce Coleman Inc.: 9
© Merlin D. Tuttle/Bat Conservation International, The National Audubon Society Collection/Photo Researchers: 20
© Michael Fogden/Bruce Coleman Inc.: 13
© Rexford Lord, The National Audubon Society Collection/Photo Researchers: 23
© Robert and Linda Mitchell: 15, 26
© Roger Rageot/David Liebman: 10, 19, 29
© Stephen Dalton, The National Audubon Society Collection/Photo Researchers: cover
© Tom McHugh, The National Audubon Society Collection/Photo Researchers: 16

On the cover...

Front cover: This vampire bat is hanging in a dark cave.
Page 2: You can easily see this vampire bat's sharp teeth.

Table of Contents

On a warm, dark night, a cow stands in a grassy field. She hangs her head down as she sleeps. Suddenly, a little animal flies through the air and lands softly on the cow's back. It crawls around a little, and then bites the cow with its sharp teeth. The bite is so small that the cow doesn't even wake up. As the cow's blood seeps out of the bite mark, the little animal licks it up with its long tongue. What is this strange creature? It's a vampire bat!

What Are Vampire Bats?

Vampire bats belong to a group of animals called **mammals.** A mammal is an animal that has hair and warm blood. Mammal mothers feed their babies with milk from their bodies. Cows, dogs, bears, and people are examples of mammals. Of all the mammals, however, only bats can fly!

These vampire bats are getting ready to hunt for their dinner. ⇒

Like all bats, vampire bats have wings that are covered with skin. Even though the skin is thin, it is very strong. The wings are attached to long fingers in the vampire bat's hand. On the vampire bat's thumb is a long claw. This claw helps the bat move and climb.

These vampire bats are crawling through a hole in a cave in Mexico. ⇒

Vampire bats got their name from a scary story. Long ago, a story started about a monster that would bite people and drink their blood. This monster was called a vampire. In real life, there are no vampires. But certain bats that bite animals and drink their blood were called vampire bats.

What Do Vampire Bats Look Like?

Vampire bats look a lot like other bats. They have small brown bodies and tiny, pointed ears. They have little feet with sharp claws. Vampire bats also have round eyes and very sharp teeth. Near its nose, a vampire bat has a small, wrinkled patch of skin. This is called a **nose leaf.**

This vampire bat lives in Costa Rica. ⇒

Where Do Vampire Bats Live?

Vampire bats live only in Central and South America. They like to live in dark caves or deep in hollow trees. A single deep, dark cave can be home to thousands of vampire bats!

Vampire bats are **nocturnal.** This means they are awake at night and sleep during the day. During the hot mornings and afternoons, vampire bats hang upside down while they sleep. When the sun goes down, the bats wake up and fly into the night to hunt for food.

⇐ Vampire bats like these use their strong feet to hang upside down.

How Do Vampire Bats Hunt?

Vampire bats are great hunters. Their long claws make it easy to climb the sides of trees and caves. When they drop to the ground, they can jump and run very fast. In the air they are powerful and silent fliers.

This vampire bat is crawling on a blanket. ⇒

Since vampire bats hunt at night, they often cannot see their food. To find their way around in the dark, vampire bats use something called **echolocation.** As they fly, the bats make high squeaks. The squeaks are so high that people cannot even hear them! The squeaks bounce off things and return to the bats as echoes.

By listening to the echoes, vampire bats can tell if they are flying near a cow, a person, a tree, or even another vampire bat! Many people believe that bats are blind. That is not true. In fact, their eyes and sense of smell are very well developed.

⇐ If you look closely, you can see this bat's bones through its wings.

What Do Vampire Bats Eat?

Vampire bats eat only one thing—blood! They use their great hunting abilities to find sleeping animals. When a vampire bat sees its victim, or **prey,** it lands on it or somewhere nearby. Since the vampire bat is so small, it can climb over a sleeping animal and not wake it up. The vampire bat then looks for a spot on the animal that does not have much hair.

This chicken doesn't even know that a vampire bat is feeding on its leg. ⇒

Once the vampire bat has found a spot, it uses its sharp teeth to bite a tiny hole in the prey's skin. As the blood oozes out, the bat licks it up. Vampire bats drink only a small amount of blood. In fact, until it wakes up, the prey animal might even not know the vampire bat was there!

Vampire bats are the only kind of bat that eats blood. Other bats eat things such as insects or small animals. Some bats also eat fruit.

⇐ This vampire bat is licking blood from a sleeping sea lion.

How Are Baby Vampire Bats Born?

A baby vampire bat is very small when it is born. It doesn't have any hair, and it depends on its mother to keep it safe and warm. With its strong legs and wings, the baby bat holds on to its mother. When it is hungry, the baby drinks milk from the mother's body.

When the baby is old enough, it climbs on its mother's back and they fly out of the cave together. For almost a year, the mother teaches her baby how to fly and hunt.

⇐ This female is protecting the baby clinging to her belly.

Are Vampire Bats Dangerous?

By itself, a vampire bat does not drink enough blood to hurt anything. Sometimes, though, dozens of vampire bats bite an animal in one night. If this happens, the animal can become very weak or sick.

The biggest problem with vampire bats is that they can carry a sickness called **rabies.** When a vampire bat has rabies, it can pass the sickness on to the other animals it bites.

This vampire bat still has blood on its tongue from its last meal. ⇒

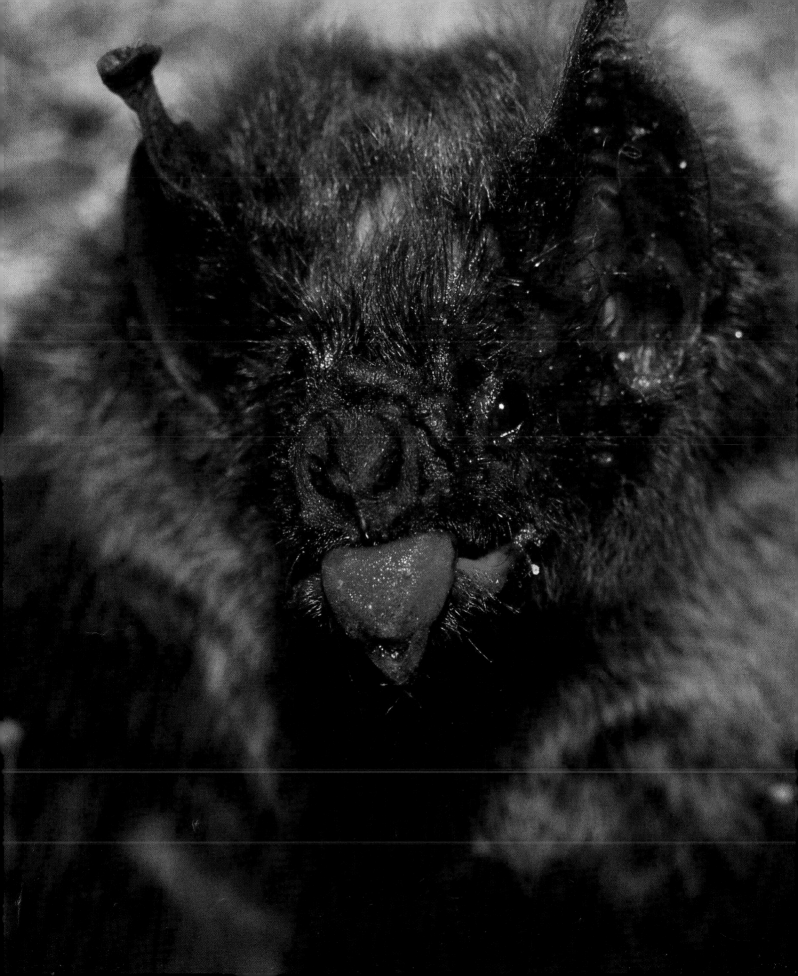

Do Vampire Bats Have Enemies?

Some animals like to eat bats. Hawks, owls, mice, skunks, and even snakes will eat bats—if they can catch them. However, the biggest enemy to vampire bats is people. Many people are afraid of vampire bats and try to kill them. Others think that all vampire bats carry rabies and try to get rid of them. They are mistaken. Only a few bats carry rabies.

People are afraid of vampire bats because they don't know about them. They are not mean, they are just trying to live and raise their babies. It's important that we try and understand the vampire bat, because it is truly one of nature's strangest and most wonderful animals.

⇐ This vampire bat lives in Belize.

Glossary

echolocation (ek–koh–loh–KAY–shun)
Echolocation is the way a vampire bat finds things in the dark. By making squeaks and listening to echoes, vampire bats can find things without seeing them.

mammals (MA–mullz)
Mammals are animals that have hair and feed their babies with milk from their bodies. Cows, dogs, and vampire bats are all mammals.

nocturnal (nok–TUR–null)
A nocturnal animal is active at night and sleeps during the day. Vampire bats are nocturnal.

nose leaf (NOHZ LEEF)
A nose leaf is a piece of skin that covers a vampire bat's nose.

prey (PRAY)
An animal that other animals hunt and eat for food is called prey.

rabies (RAY-beez)
Rabies is a dangerous sickness that some animals carry. Some vampire bats carry rabies.

Web Sites

Learn more about vampire bats:

http://www.seaworld.org/animal_bytes/vampire_batab.html

http://animaldiversity.ummz.umich.edu/accounts/desmodus/d._rotundus

http://www.tower.org/menagerie/safari/vampirebat.html

http://www.scz.org/animals/mam-ind.html

Index